Leveled Texts

For First Grade

Consultants

Kristy Stark, M.A.Ed.
Reading Level Consultant
Long Beach, California

Wendy Conklin, M.A.
Gifted Education Consultant
Round Rock, Texas

Dennis Benjamin
Special Education Consultant
Prince William County Public Schools, Virginia

Marcela von Vacano
English Language Learner Consultant
Arlington County Schools, Virginia

Publishing Credits

Corinne Burton, M.A.Ed., *President*; Conni Medina, M.A.Ed., *Managing Editor*;
Emily Rossman Smith, M.A.Ed., *Content Director*; Angela Johnson, M.F.A., M.S.Ed., *Editor*;
Robin Erickson, *Multimedia Designer*; Kevin Pham, *Production Artist*;
Danielle Deovlet, *Assistant Editor*

Image Credits

pp.17, 19, 21 TheoSid/Bigstock; pp.83, 85, 87 The Washington Post/Getty Images;
pp.101, 103, 105 Kelly Redinger/Designpics; pp.111, 113, 115 Fancy/Alamy;
pp.125, 127, 129 Blend Images/Alamy; All other images from iStock, Shutterstock, or the
public domain.

Standards

© 2004 Mid-continent Research for Education and Learning (McREL)
© 2006 Teachers of English to Speakers of Other Languages, Inc. (TESOL)
© Copyright 2010. National Governors Association Center for Best Practices and Council of
Chief State School Officers. All rights reserved.

Shell Education

A division of Teacher Created Materials
5301 Oceanus Drive
Huntington Beach, CA 92649–1030
http://www.tcmpub.com/shell-education
ISBN 978–1–4258–1628–5
©2016 Shell Educational Publishing, Inc.

Table of Contents

What Is Differentiation?

Over the past few years, classrooms have evolved into diverse pools of learners. Gifted students, English language learners, special-needs students, high achievers, underachievers, and average students all come together to learn from one teacher. The teacher is expected to meet their diverse needs in one classroom. It brings back memories of the one-room schoolhouse during early American history. Not too long ago, lessons were designed to be one size fits all. It was thought that students in the same grade learned in similar ways. Today, teachers know that viewpoint to be faulty. Students have different learning styles, come from different cultures, experience a variety of emotions, and have varied interests. For each subject, they also differ in academic readiness. At times, the challenges teachers face can be overwhelming, as they struggle to figure out how to create learning environments that address the differences they find in their students.

What is differentiation? Carol Ann Tomlinson (2014, 1) describes the challenge of differentiation as reaching out to "students who span the spectrum of learning readiness, personal interests, and culturally shaped ways of seeing and speaking about and experiencing the world." Differentiation can be carried out by any teacher who keeps the learners at the forefront of his or her instruction. The effective teacher asks, "What am I going to do to shape instruction to meet the needs of all my learners?" One method or methodology will not reach all students.

Differentiation encompasses what is taught, how it is taught, and the products students create to show what they have learned. When differentiating curriculum, teachers become the organizers of learning opportunities within the classroom environment. These categories are often referred to as content, process, and product.

- **Content:** Differentiating the content means to put more depth into the curriculum through organizing the curriculum concepts and structure of knowledge.

- **Process:** Differentiating the process requires the use of varied instructional techniques and materials to enhance the learning of students.

- **Product:** When products are differentiated, cognitive development and the students' abilities to express themselves improve.

Teachers should differentiate content, process, and products according to students' characteristics. These characteristics include students' readiness, learning styles, and interests.

- **Readiness:** If a learning experience aligns closely with students' previous skills and understanding of a topic, they will learn better.

- **Learning styles:** Teachers should create assignments that allow students to complete work according to their personal preferences and styles.

- **Interests:** If a topic sparks excitement in the learners, then students will become involved in learning and better remember what is taught.

How to Differentiate Using This Product

The leveled texts in this series help teachers differentiate language arts, mathematics, science, and social studies content for students. Each section has five passages, and each passage is written at three different reading levels. (See page 8 for more information.) While these texts are written on three reading levels, all levels remain strong in presenting subject-specific content and vocabulary. Teachers can focus on the same content standard or objective for the whole class, but individual students can access the content at their instructional levels rather than at their frustration levels.

Determining your students' instructional reading levels is the first step in the process. It is important to assess their reading abilities often so students are instructed on the correct levels. Below are suggested ways to use this resource, as well as other resources in your building, to determine students' reading levels.

- **Running records:** While your class is doing independent work, pull your below-grade-level students aside, one at a time. Individually, have them read aloud the lowest level of a text from this product (the circle level) as you record any errors they make on your own copy of the text. Assess their accuracy and fluency by marking the words they say incorrectly and listening for fluent reading. Use your judgment to determine whether students seem frustrated as they read. Following the reading, ask comprehension questions to assess their understanding of the material. If students read accurately and fluently and comprehend the material, move them up to the next level and repeat the process. As a general guideline, students reading below 90% accuracy are likely to feel frustrated as they read. There are also a variety of published reading assessment tools that can be used to assess students' reading levels using the oral running record format.

- **Refer to other resources:** You can also use other reading level placement tests, such as the Developmental Reading Assessment or the Qualitative Reading Inventory, to determine your students' reading levels. Then, use the chart on page 8 to determine which text level is the best fit for each student.

Teachers can also use the texts in this series to scaffold the content for their students. At the beginning of the year, students at the lowest reading levels may need focused teacher guidance. As the year progresses, teachers can begin giving students multiple levels of the same text to allow them to work independently to improve their comprehension. This means that each student would have a copy of the text at his or her independent reading level and a copy of the text one level above that. As students read the instructional-level texts, they can use the lower texts to better understand the difficult vocabulary. By scaffolding the content in this way, teachers can support students as they move up through the reading levels. This will encourage students to work with texts that are closer to the grade level at which they will be tested.

General Information About Student Populations

Below-Grade-Level Students

As with all student populations, students who are below grade level span a spectrum of abilities. Some of these students have individualized education plans, while others do not. Some below-grade-level students are English language learners (ELLs), while others are native English speakers. Selected students receive intervention and/or support services, while many other students do not qualify for such services. The shift toward inclusive classrooms has caused an increase in the number of below-grade-level students in the general education classrooms.

These students, regardless of abilities, are often evaluated on the same learning objectives as their on-grade-level peers, and their learning becomes the responsibility of classroom teachers. The following questions come to mind: How do classroom teachers provide this population with "access to texts that allows them to perform like good, proficient readers" (Fountas and Pinnell 2012, 2)? How do classroom teachers differentiate for this population without limiting access to content, grade-level vocabulary, and language? Pages 132–136 give tangible strategies to support this student population.

On-Grade-Level Students

Often, on-grade-level students get overlooked when planning curriculum. More emphasis is placed on students who struggle and, at times, on those students who excel. Teachers spend time teaching basic skills and even go below grade level to ensure that all students are up to speed. While this is a noble thing and is necessary at times, in the midst of it all, the on-grade-level students can get lost in the shuffle. Providing activities that are too challenging can frustrate these students, and on the other hand, assignments that are too easy can seem tedious. The key to reaching this population successfully is to find the right level of activities and questions while keeping a keen eye on their diverse learning styles. Strategies can include designing activities based on the theory of multiple intelligences. Current brain research points to the success of active learning strategies. These strategies provoke strong positive emotions and use movement during the learning process to help these students learn more effectively. On-grade-level students also benefit from direct teaching of higher-level thinking skills. Keep the activities open ended so that these students can surprise you with all they know. The strategies described on pages 137–138 were specifically chosen because they are very effective for meeting the needs of on-grade-level students.

General Information About Student Populations

Above-Grade-Level Students

All students should be learning, growing, and expanding their knowledge in school. This includes above-grade-level students, too. But they will not grow and learn unless someone challenges them with appropriate curriculum. In her book *Differentiating the Language Arts for High Ability Learners*, Joyce Van Tassel-Baska (2003, 2) stresses that "the level of curriculum for gifted learners must be adapted to their needs for advancement, depth, and complexity." Doing this can be overwhelming at times, even for experienced teachers. However, there are some strategies that teachers can use to challenge the gifted population. These strategies include open-ended questions, student-directed learning, and extension assignments. See pages 139–140 for more information about each of these strategies.

English Language Learners

Acquiring a second language is a lengthy process that integrates listening, speaking, reading, and writing. Students who are newcomers to the English language are not able to deeply process information until they have mastered a certain number of language structures and vocabulary words. Even after mastering these structures, English language learners need to be immersed in rich verbal and textual language daily in school. Students may learn social language in one or two years. However, academic language takes up to eight years for most students to learn. Teaching academic language requires good planning and effective implementation. Pacing, or the rate at which information is presented, is another important component in this process. English language learners need to hear the same words in context several times, and they need to practice structures to internalize the words. Reviewing and summarizing what was taught are absolutely necessary for English language learners' success in the future (August and Shanahan 2006). See pages 141–143 for more information about each of the strategies mentioned here.

7

How to Use This Product

Readability Chart

Title of the Text	Circle	Square	Triangle
Animal Parents and Babies	labels	1.4	3.2
Shapes	labels	1.9	3.1
Playing Sports	labels	1.7	3.2
Grandpa and Me	labels	1.4	3.4
Homes Around the World	labels	1.5	3.1
Crafty Kids	labels	1.4	3.2
Getting Ready for School	labels	1.2	3.0
Our Favorite Sports	labels	1.8	3.0
Birthday Time!	labels	1.8	3.3
Looking at Animals	labels	1.8	3.9
Plenty of Plants!	labels	1.5	3.6
The Seasons	labels	1.8	3.8
How Sound Moves	labels	1.3	3.0
Light Makes a Rainbow	labels	1.2	3.2
Tools	labels	1.3	3.4
Be Fair!	labels	1.4	3.6
Money	labels	1.5	3.0
Jobs Around Town	labels	1.8	3.6
Getting Around School	labels	1.1	3.3
Happy 4th of July, America!	labels	1.9	3.7

Correlation to Standards

The Every Student Succeeds Act (ESSA) mandates that all states adopt challenging academic standards that help students meet the goal of college and career readiness. While many states already adopted academic standards prior to ESSA, the act continues to hold states accountable for detailed and comprehensive standards.

Shell Education is committed to producing educational materials that are research and standards based. In this effort, all products are correlated to the academic standards of the 50 states, the District of Columbia, and the Department of Defense Dependent Schools. Shell Education uses the Mid-continent Research for Education and Learning (McREL) Compendium to create standards correlations. Each year, McREL analyzes state standards and revises the compendium. By following this procedure, they are able to produce a general compilation of national standards. A correlation report customized for your state can be printed directly from the following website: **www.tcmpub.com/administrators/correlations/**.

How to Use This Product *(cont.)*

Components of the Product

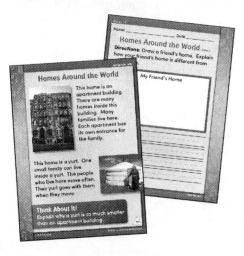

The Leveled Texts

- There are 20 topics in this book. Each topic is leveled to three different reading levels. The images and fonts used for each level within a topic are the same.

- Behind each page number, you'll see a shape. These shapes indicate the reading levels of each piece so that you can make sure students are working with the correct texts. The circle level pieces have images only with no text so they can be used by nonreaders. The square level pieces are for very early readers and use labels only. See the chart on page 8 for the specific level of each triangle text.

labels	Levels 1.2–1.9	Levels 3.0-3.9

Comprehension Questions

- Each text includes a comprehension question. They are written to allow all students to be successful within a whole-class discussion. The questions are closely linked so that teachers can ask multiple questions on the topics and all students will be able to participate in the conversations about the texts.

Comprehension Activities

- Each level of the texts also includes a comprehension activity. Like the texts, the comprehension activities were created with nonreaders and early readers in mind. The below-grade-level students might focus on the images, while the above-grade-level students can delve deeper into the meanings of the sentences and images.

9

How to Use This Product *(cont.)*

Tips for Managing the Product

How to Prepare the Texts

- When you copy these texts, be sure you set your copier to copy photographs. Run a few test pages and adjust the contrast as necessary. If you want the students to be able to appreciate the images, you will need to carefully prepare the texts for them.

- You also have full-color versions of the texts provided in PDF form on the Digital Resource CD. (See page 144 for more information.) Depending on how many copies you need to make, printing full-color versions and/or copying from a full-color version might work best for you.

- Keep in mind that you should copy two-sided to two-sided if you pull the pages out of the book. The shapes behind the page numbers will help you keep the pages organized as you prepare them.

Distributing the Texts

- Some teachers wonder about how to hand out the texts within one classroom. They worry that students will feel insulted if they do not get the same papers as their neighbors. The first step in dealing with these texts is to set up your classroom as a place where all students learn at their individual instructional levels. Making this clear as a fact of life in your classroom is key. Otherwise, the students may constantly ask about why their work is different. You do not need to get into the technicalities of the reading levels. Just state it as a fact that every student will not be working on the same assignment every day. If you do this, then passing out the varied levels is not a problem. Just pass them to the correct students as you circle the room.

- If you would rather not have students openly aware of the differences in the texts, you can try these strategies for passing out the materials.

  - Make a pile in your hands from the circle to triangle level. Put your fingers between the levels. As you approach each student, you pull from the correct section to meet his/her reading level. If you do not hesitate too much in front of each desk, the students will probably not notice.

  - Begin the class period with an opening activity. Put the texts in different places around the room. As students work quietly, circulate and direct students to the correct locations for retrieving the texts you want them to use.

  - Organize the texts in small piles by seating arrangement so that when you arrive at a group of desks you will have just the levels you need.

Animal Parents and Babies

penguins and an egg

hen and chicks

Think About It!
Which animals are the parents?

Name: _____ Date: _____

Animal Parents and Babies (cont.)

Directions: Draw a picture of an animal parent and baby. Label your picture.

Animal Parents and Babies

A father penguin warms the egg.

A mother hen shows her chicks how to peck.

Think About It!
How do parents help their babies?

13

Name: _____ Date: _____

Animal Parents and Babies (cont.)

Directions: Draw a picture of an animal parent and baby. Write about your picture.

_____
- -
_____
_____
- -
_____

Animal Parents and Babies

Penguin fathers keep their babies safe before they hatch. They protect eggs from the cold. An egg cannot touch the ice, so the father balances the egg on his feet for two months.

Animal mothers teach their babies. Here, a mother hen teaches her chicks to peck. They hunt and peck for food to eat.

Think About It!
Why do baby animals need their parents?

Name: _____ Date: _____

Animal Parents and Babies (cont.)

Directions: Draw a picture of an animal parent and baby. Write about your picture.

Shapes

wheel

circle

blocks

squares

Think About It!

How many sides does a square have?

Name: _____ Date: _____

Shapes *(cont.)*

Directions: Draw three shapes that you see around you. Label each shape.

Shapes

This wheel is shaped like a circle, so it can roll smoothly over the ground.

The sides of a block are squares so they can sit in place. They can also be stacked!

Think About It!
Name one way a circle and square are different.

Name: _____ Date: _____

Shapes *(cont.)*

Directions: Draw three shapes that you see around you. Write about each shape.

Shapes

Shapes are located all around us. What shape do you see in this picture? This wheel is shaped like a circle, so it can roll smoothly over the ground. People use wheels on things such as cars and wagons to help move large things.

What shapes do you see in this picture? The sides of these blocks are shaped like squares so they sit in place. They can also be stacked because every side is flat. Look around you to locate more shapes hidden in everyday things.

Think About It!

What shapes can be made if you cut a square in half?

21

Name: _____ Date: _____

Shapes (cont.)

Directions: Draw a picture of your classroom using only circles, squares, and rectangles. Describe what you notice about shapes in your classroom.

- -

- -

- -

Playing Sports

basketball

soccer

Think About It!
Which sport do you play by kicking a ball with your feet?

Name: _____ Date: _____

Playing Sports (cont.)

Directions: Draw a picture of your favorite sport. Label your picture.

Playing Sports

In basketball, players earn points when they shoot the ball through a basket. Can you shoot a ball? Then maybe basketball is the sport for you.

Soccer takes quick feet. Soccer players use their feet to kick the ball. If you have quick feet, try soccer.

Think About It!
How are basketball and soccer different?

Name: _____ Date: _____

Playing Sports (cont.)

Directions: Draw a picture of your favorite sport. Explain why that is your favorite sport.

Playing Sports

In basketball, players earn points when they shoot the ball through a basket. If you can shoot a ball, then maybe basketball is the sport for you.

Soccer requires speedy feet. Soccer players use their feet to kick the ball around the field. If you have quick feet, give soccer a try.

Think About It!
What other body parts are used to play sports?

Name: _____ Date: _____

Playing Sports *(cont.)*

Directions: Describe how your favorite sport helps to keep you fit and healthy. Draw a picture to show this.

Grandpa and Me

We walk.

We read.

Think About It!
What do the boy and grandpa do together?

Name: _____ Date: _____

Grandpa and Me (cont.)

Directions: Draw pictures of what the boy and grandpa do together. Label each picture.

Grandpa and Me

Grandpa and
I walk to
the park.

Then we walk
over to the
bookstore.

Think About It!
What is different about what the
boy and grandpa choose to read?

31

Name: _____ Date: _____

Grandpa and Me (cont.)

Directions: Draw a picture for a place the boy and grandpa stop on their walk. Write about your picture.

Grandpa and Me

Grandpa is here to pick me up for our Saturday walk. First, we walk outside and head to our favorite park. We see all kinds of animals and enjoy being outside.

Next, we walk to the bookstore. We each pick out something interesting to read. When we are finished, we walk back home.

Think About It!
In what ways are the boy and his grandpa similar?

33

Name: _____ Date: _____

Grandpa and Me (cont.)

Directions: Draw a picture of another place that the boy and his grandpa could go. Describe why they like going to this new place.

_____

- -

_____

_____

- -

_____

Homes Around the World

apartment

yurt

Think About It!
Which home can hold more people?

Name: _____ Date: _____

Homes Around the World *(cont.)*

Directions: Draw a picture of your home. Label the type of home you live in.

_____

- -

_____

Homes Around the World

This home is an apartment building.

This home is a yurt.

Think About It!

How are an apartment building and a yurt similar? How are they different?

© Shell Education   51628—*Leveled Texts for First Grade*

Name: _____ Date: _____

Homes Around the World (cont.)

Directions: Draw a picture of your home. Write a sentence about the type of home you live in.

_____

_____

_____

Homes Around the World

This home is an apartment building. There are many homes inside this building. Many families live here. Every apartment has its own living space each family.

This home is a yurt. One small family is able to live inside a yurt. The people who live here move often. Their yurt goes with them when they move.

Think About It!
Explain why a yurt is so much smaller than an apartment building.

39

Name: _____ Date: _____

Homes Around the World (cont.)

Directions: Draw a friend's home. Explain how your friend's home is different from your home.

My Friend's Home

_____

- -

_____

- -

_____

- -

_____

- -

Crafty Kids

picture frames

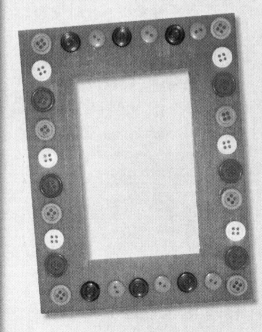

patterns

Think About It!
What do the students use to make patterns on the frames?

Name: _____ Date: _____

Crafty Kids *(cont.)*

Directions: Draw a pattern on the picture frame below. Label your pattern.

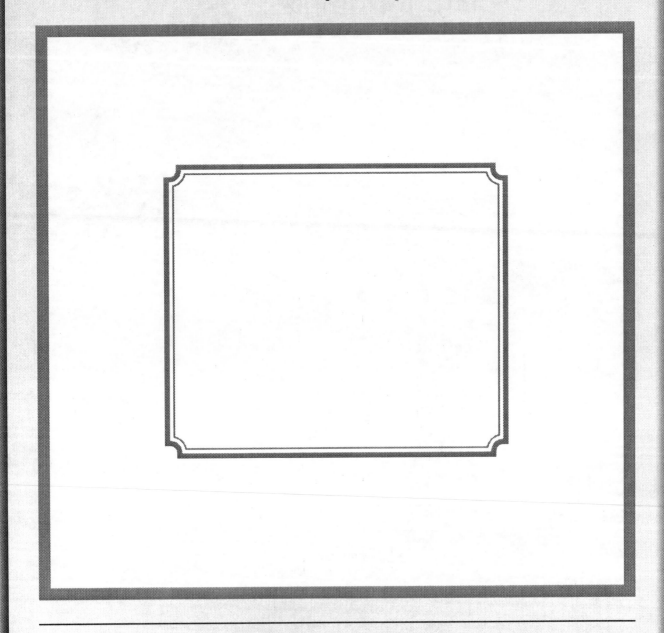

_____

- -

_____

Crafty Kids

Miss Lee's class makes picture frames.

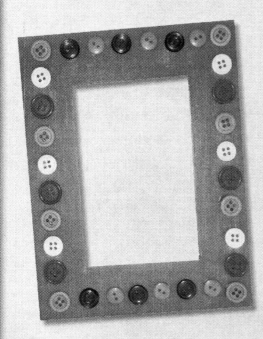

The students make patterns on the frames.

Think About It!
The picture frame with buttons has two patterns. Explain each pattern.

43

Name: _____ Date: _____

Crafty Kids *(cont.)*

Directions: Draw a pattern on the picture frame below. Write a sentence about your pattern.

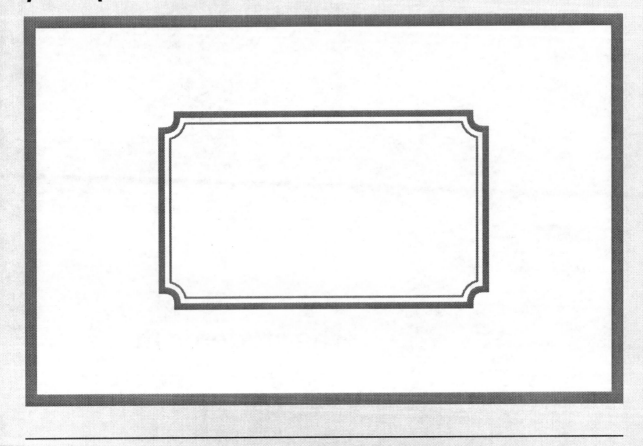

_____

- -

_____

_____

- -

_____

_____

Crafty Kids

The students will sell crafts to raise money for their school. Miss Lee's class is crafting picture frames. The students want the frames to look attractive for the people who will buy them.

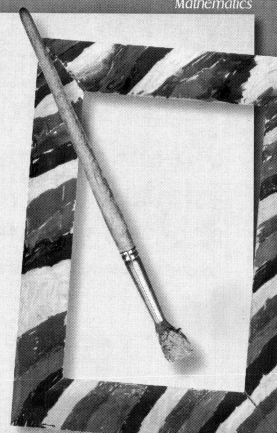

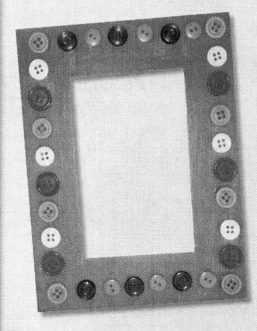

The students use buttons to create patterns on the frames. They also make patterns with paint. The students think people will want to purchase their frames.

Think About It!

How are the paint and button patterns similar? How are the patterns different?

Name: _____ Date: _____

Crafty Kids *(cont.)*

Directions: Draw a pattern on the picture frame below. Write a few sentences about your pattern.

Getting Ready for School

cereal and juice

bread with
peanut butter

Think About It!
What do the kids eat for breakfast?

Name: _____ Date: _____

Getting Ready for School (cont.)

Directions: Draw four pictures to show how you get ready for school. Label each picture.

Getting Ready for School

Rod eats some cereal. He drinks a glass of juice.

Tia eats bread with peanut butter.

Think About It!

How are the two kids similar in how they get ready for school? How do they get ready differently?

49

Name: _____ Date: _____

Getting Ready for School (cont.)

Directions: Draw four pictures to show the order in which you get ready for school. Write about getting ready for school.

Getting Ready for School

Rod's mom wakes him up in the morning. After he gets dressed, he makes and eats a bowl of cereal. He also drinks a glass of orange juice.

Tia's dad wakes her up for school each morning. For breakfast, she eats bread with peanut butter. She spreads the peanut butter onto the bread with a knife. She then washes her dishes when she is done. Tia gets dressed and leaves for school.

Think About It!
Compare how you get ready for school with how Tia and Rod get ready.

Name: _____ Date: _____

Getting Ready for School (cont.)

Directions: Draw four pictures to show the order in which you get ready for school. Explain the steps involved in getting ready for school.

Our Favorite Sports

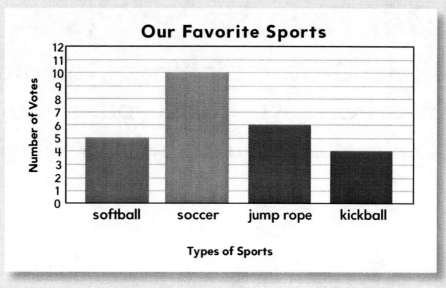

sports graph

Think About It!
What sports are shown?

 51628—Leveled Texts for First Grade

Name: _____ Date: _____

Our Favorite Sports *(cont.)*

Directions: Draw a picture of you playing your favorite sport. Label your picture.

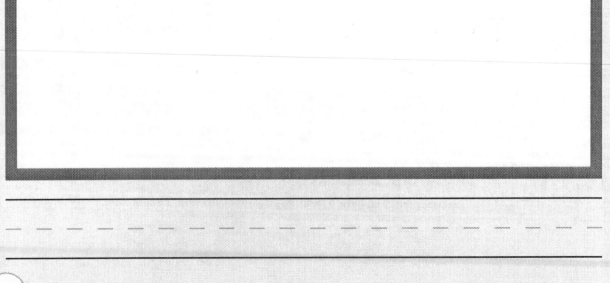

_____

- -

_____

Our Favorite Sports

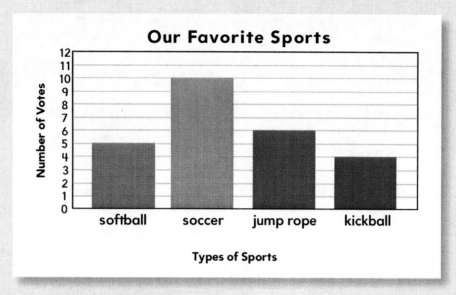

We vote on sports. Then we make a graph to show the most popular sports in our classroom.

Think About It!
Which sport got the most votes?

Name: _____ Date: _____

Our Favorite Sports (cont.)

Directions: Draw a picture of you playing your favorite sport. Explain why it is your favorite sport.

Our Favorite Sports

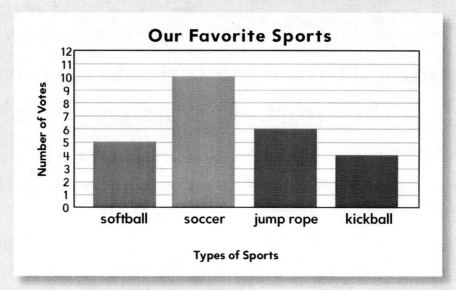

In our class, we like to play different sports. We vote on which sports are our favorites. We choose four different sports: soccer, softball, jump rope, and kickball.

Then, we make a bar graph to show our votes. This type of graph uses bars to show data. The length of each bar is affected by how many people like the sport.

Think About It!
Which sport did kids like the least? How do you know this?

57

Name: _____ Date: _____

Our Favorite Sports *(cont.)*

Directions: Draw a picture of you playing your favorite sport. Explain how to play this sport.

Birthday Time!

Josh and Jen

good friends

Josh's Friends
Jamie
Dawson
Han
Hunter

Jen's Friends
Rori
Veronica
Allie
Juan

Think About It!
How many good friends do Josh and Jen have?

Name: _____ Date: _____

Birthday Time! *(cont.)*

Directions: Draw a picture of a birthday party you have had or would like to have. Label your picture.

Birthday Time!

Josh and Jen are twins. They plan their birthday party together.

They can each invite four friends.

Josh's Friends
Jamie

Dawson

Han

Hunter

Jen's Friends
Rori

Veronica

Allie

Juan

Think About It!
How many kids will be at the party in total?

Name: _____ Date: _____

Birthday Time! *(cont.)*

Directions: Draw a picture of a birthday party you have had or would like to have. Write about your picture.

51628—Leveled Texts for First Grade

Birthday Time!

Josh and Jen are twins. Since they have the same birthday, their mom is allowing them to plan their birthday party together.

They can each invite four friends. They combine their lists to invite eight friends total.

Josh's Friends
Jamie
Dawson
Han
Hunter

Jen's Friends
Rori
Veronica
Allie
Juan

Think About It!
Why do you think Josh and Jen invite the same number of friends?

63

Name: _____ Date: _____

Birthday Time! *(cont.)*

Directions: Imagine you are planning your birthday party. Write your plan, including who you will invite and what things you will need for your party.

_____

_____

_____

_____

_____

_____

_____

_____

_____

_____

Looking at Animals

python
snake

long in length

Think About It!
Is a python long or short?

Name: _____ Date: _____

Looking at Animals (cont.)

Directions: Draw a picture of your favorite animal. Label your picture.

_____

- -

_____

Looking at Animals

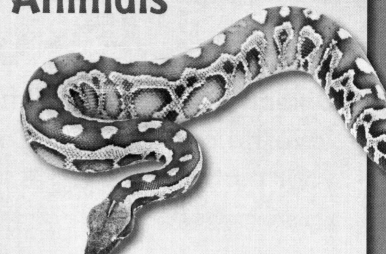

A python is a type of snake.

An adult python can get to be the same length as a man.

Think About It!

Describe a python.

Name: _____ Date: _____

Looking at Animals (cont.)

Directions: Draw a picture of your favorite animal. Write a sentence about your picture.

_____
- -
_____
_____
- -
_____

Looking at Animals

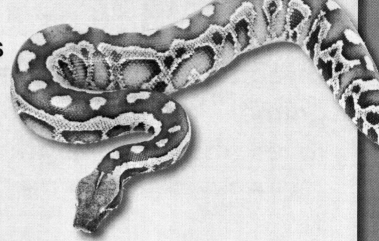

The python moves by stretching out, bunching up its middle, and then pushing its head forward.

An adult python can grow to be quite long. If a grown man could lie down next to it, they would be close to the same length!

Think About It!
Explain how pythons and people are similar. How are they different?

Name: _____ Date: _____

Looking at Animals (cont.)

Directions: Draw a picture of your favorite animal. Write about your picture. Be sure to tell about the length of the animal.

Plenty of Plants!

plants

carrots and spinach

Think About It!
Name a type of plant.

Name: _____ Date: _____

Plenty of Plants! *(cont.)*

Directions: Draw a picture of a plant you have seen. Label your picture.

Plenty of Plants!

Plants grow all around us.

Carrots and spinach are types of plants that we can eat.

Think About It!
Where are some places that plants grow?

73

Name: _____ Date: _____

Plenty of Plants! (cont.)

Directions: Draw a picture of a plant you have seen. Write about your picture.

Plenty of Plants!

Plants grow all around us in many shapes, sizes, and colors. Big, tall trees and short, green grass are plants.

People eat crunchy carrots and leafy spinach plants. Spinach and carrots are healthy and tasty.

Think About It!
How are all plants similar? In what ways are some plants different?

75

Name: _____ Date: _____

Plenty of Plants! *(cont.)*

Directions: Draw a picture of your favorite types of plants to eat. Explain why you like to eat those plants.

The Seasons

spring and
summer

autumn and
winter

Think About It!
Name the four seasons.

Name: _____ Date: _____

The Seasons *(cont.)*

Directions: Draw a picture of your favorite season. Label your picture.

_____

_____

The Seasons

Seasons change through the year. Spring turns to summer. Summer turns to autumn.

Autumn is also called fall. Autumn turns to winter. Then, it is spring again.

Think About It!
How are spring and summer similar?

Name: _____ Date: _____

The Seasons *(cont.)*

Directions: Draw a picture of your favorite season. Explain why it is your favorite.

The Seasons

Seasons change during the year. Spring changes to summer. Summer changes to autumn.

Autumn is also called fall. Fall becomes winter. Then, after winter, it is spring again.

Think About It!
Why might autumn also be called fall?

Name: _____ Date: _____

The Seasons (cont.)

Directions: Draw a picture of your favorite season. Explain why you like this season.

How Sound Moves

vibrate

sound waves

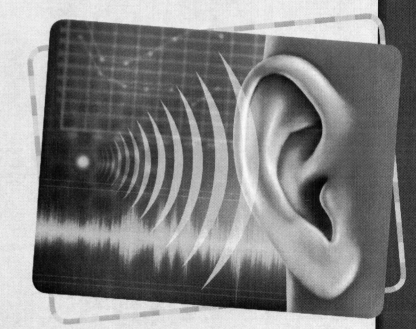

Think About It!
How does sound move?

Name: _____ Date: _____

How Sound Moves (cont.)

Directions: Draw a picture of you playing an instrument. Label your picture.

_____

_ _

_____

How Sound Moves

A drummer hits a stick against a drum. This makes it vibrate. To vibrate is to move back and forth quickly.

Vibrations bump the air and start sound waves. The sound waves move through the air to your ear.

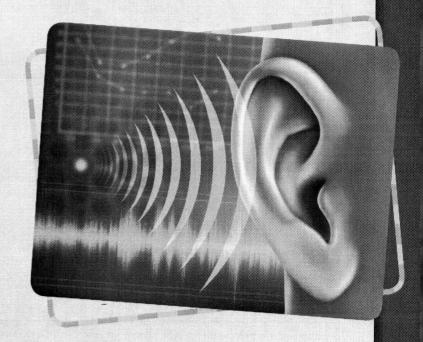

Think About It!
What does *vibrate* mean?

Name: _____ Date: _____

How Sound Moves (cont.)

Directions: Draw a picture of you playing an instrument. Write about the instrument.

_____

_____

_____

_____

How Sound Moves

A drummer hits a drumstick against a drumhead to make it vibrate. To vibrate is to move back and forth quickly.

The vibrations bump the air and start sound waves. The sound waves travel through the air to your ear.

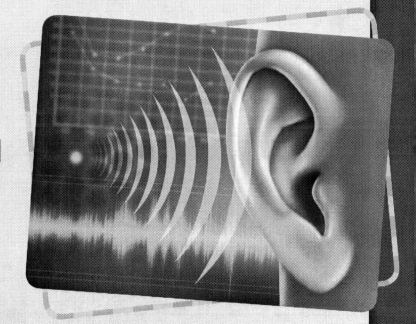

Think About It!

What other sense can be used to detect vibrations?

87

Name: _____ Date: _____

How Sound Moves (cont.)

Directions: Draw a picture of you playing an instrument. Explain how sound travels from the instrument to your ears.

_____
_____
_____
_____
_____

Light Makes a Rainbow

rain and sun

rainbow

light bends

Think About It!
What makes a rainbow?

Name: _____ Date: _____

Light Makes a Rainbow (cont.)

Directions: Draw a rainbow. Label your picture.

Light Makes a Rainbow

Rain and sun make a rainbow.

Light goes through water drops. The light bends into colors.

Think About It!
How are rainbows made?

 51628—*Leveled Texts for First Grade*

Name: _____ Date: _____

Light Makes a Rainbow *(cont.)*

Directions: Draw a picture of you looking out your window at a rainbow. Write about your picture.

Light Makes a Rainbow

Rain and sun make a rainbow.

A rainbow happens when light passes through water drops and the light bends. The bend in the light causes it to split into colors.

Think About It!

Explain how sun and rain work together to make a rainbow.

Name: _____ Date: _____

Light Makes a Rainbow (cont.)

Directions: Draw a picture of you looking out your window at a rainbow. Write a story to go with your picture.

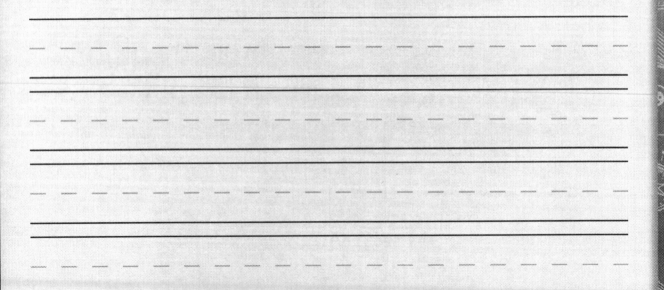

Tools

**telescope
(TEH-luh-skope)**

**microscope
(MY-kruh-skope)**

Think About It!
What is a tool?

Name: _____ Date: _____

Tools (cont.)

Directions: Draw a picture of a tool you have used. Label your picture.

Tools

A telescope (TEH-luh-skope) is a tool. It helps us see things that are far away. It can even see into space!

A microscope (MY-kruh-skope) is a tool, too. It helps us see things that are too small to see with just our eyes. It makes small things look big and clear.

Think About It!
Which tool should you use if you want to see space? Why?

97

Name: _____ Date: _____

Tools *(cont.)*

Directions: Draw a picture of a tool you have used. Explain how you used the tool.

Tools

A telescope (TEH-luh-skope) is a tool that helps us see far away things. It can even see into space!

A microscope (MY-kruh-skope) is a tool that helps us see things that are too small to see with just our eyes. It makes small things look bigger and helps us see them clearly.

Think About It!
How do tools help people learn about the world?

99

Name: _____ Date: _____

Tools (cont.)

Directions: Draw a picture of a tool you have used. Explain why that tool is useful.

Be Fair!

fair

equal

Think About It!
What is one way to show that you are being fair?

Name: _____ Date: _____

Be Fair! *(cont.)*

Directions: One way to be fair is to follow the rules. Draw a picture of a game that has rules. Label your picture.

_____

_____

Be Fair!

When you are fair, you treat people the same.

You give everyone the equal chances.

Think About It!
What does it mean to give everyone the same chances?

Name: _____ Date: _____

Be Fair! *(cont.)*

Directions: One way to be fair is to follow the rules. Draw a picture of a game that has rules. Write about your picture.

_____

_____

_____

_____

Be Fair!

When you are fair, you treat each person the same as all other people.

You give everyone an equal chance when you are fair.

Think About It!
Explain why it is important for everyone to be fair.

Name: _____ Date: _____

Be Fair! (cont.)

Directions: One way to be fair is to follow the rules. Draw a picture of a game that has rules. Then write the rules of the game.

Money

money

earning money

Name: _____ Date: _____

Money *(cont.)*

Directions: Draw a picture of money. Label your picture.

_____

- -

_____

Money

People use money to pay for things.

When you work for your money, you earn it.

Think About It!

What are some jobs people can do to earn money?

Name: _____ Date: _____

Money *(cont.)*

Directions: Draw three different coins. Circle the one that has the highest value. Write about your picture.

_____

- -

_____

- -

_____

Money

People use money to pay people for their work or to buy things.

Money can be a paper bill or a coin. When you work for your money, you earn it. People can earn money by doing many different jobs.

Think About It!

Explain the relationship between money and jobs.

Name: _____ Date: _____

Money (cont.)

Directions: Draw five bills or coins in order from least to greatest value. Then describe how you can earn money.

Jobs Around Town

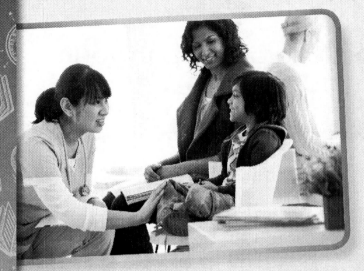

nurse

firefighters

Think About It!
How do nurses and firefighters help people?

Name: _____ Date: _____

Jobs Around Town *(cont.)*

Directions: Draw a picture of a job in your community. Label your picture.

_____

_____

Jobs Around Town

There are many types of jobs. Nurses help doctors. They take care of people.

Firefighters help people, too. They put out fires. They help to keep people safe.

Think About It!
What other jobs do people do to help others?

Name: _____ Date: _____

Jobs Around Town *(cont.)*

Directions: Draw a picture of a job at your school. Write about your picture.

Jobs Around Town

There are many jobs around town. Nurses help to take care of people. They also help doctors.

Firefighters help people, too. Firefighters put out fires. They help keep people safe.

Think About It!
Why are these jobs important to your community?

Name: _____ Date: _____

Jobs Around Town (cont.)

Directions: Draw a picture of a job in your town. Describe why that job is important.

_____

- -

_____

_____

- -

_____

_____

_____

- -

Getting Around School

school map

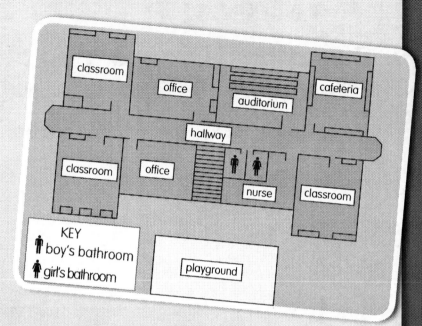

map key

Think About It!
What is a map?

Name: _____ Date: _____

Getting Around School (cont.)

Directions: Draw a map of your classroom.

Getting Around School

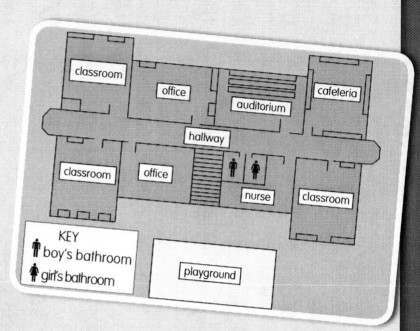

This map shows places at a school.

KEY
👨 boy's bathroom
👩 girl's bathroom

A map key tells what each symbol (SIM-buhl) that the map uses means.

Think About It!
How are map keys helpful?

© *Shell Education*

Name: _____ Date: _____

Getting Around School *(cont.)*

Directions: Draw a map of your classroom. Label things on your map.

Getting Around School

Maps can show you how to get around and find landmarks in many different places. This map shows landmarks at a school. You can use it to locate the playground.

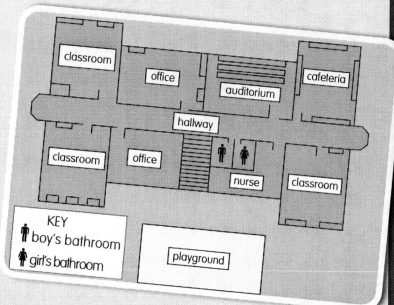

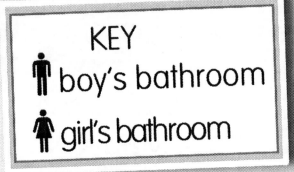

Maps use symbols (SIM-buhls). A map key defines each symbol on a map.

Think About It!
Explain what it would be like to use a map without a map key.

Name: _____ Date: _____

Getting Around School *(cont.)*

Directions: Draw a map of your classroom. Use symbols on the map. Make a map key to tell what each symbol means.

Map Key

Happy 4th of July, America!

4th of July

celebrate freedom

Think About It!
What do Americans celebrate on the 4th of July?

Name: _____ Date: _____

Happy 4th of July, America! (cont.)

Directions: Draw a picture to show how you celebrate a holiday. Label your picture.

Happy 4th of July, America!

America observes Independence Day. It falls on the fourth day of July.

Some towns have parades. At night, the sky fills with color. The air fills with sound. Fireworks are lit. This holiday marks when America became free.

Think About It!
What does *Independence* mean?

Name: _____ Date: _____

Happy 4th of July, America! *(cont.)*

Directions: Draw a picture to show how you celebrate a holiday. Write about your picture.

Happy 4th of July, America!

America celebrates Independence Day on the 4th of July. Many people celebrate outside. Some towns have parades.

At night, people light fireworks. The air fills with sound. The sky fills with color. This holiday marks when America won its freedom.

Think About It!
Explain how *freedom* and *independence* relate to each other.

129

Name: _____ Date: _____

Happy 4th of July, America! (cont.)

Directions: Draw a picture to show how you celebrate a holiday. Explain why holidays are important to you and your family.

References Cited

August, Diane and Timothy Shanahan. 2006. *Developing Literacy in Second-Language Learners: Report of the National Literacy Panel on Language-Minority Children and Youth.* Mahwah, New Jersey: Lawrence Erlbaum Associates, Inc.

Fountas, Irene and Gay Su Pinnell. 2012. *The Critical Role of Text Complexity in Teaching Children to Read.* Portsmouth, Virginia: Heinemann.

Naughton, Victoria M. 1993. "Creative Mapping for Content Reading." *Journal of Reading.* 37(4): 326.

Pearson, P. David, and Dale D. Johnson. 1978. *Teaching Reading Comprehension.* New York: Hold, Rinehart and Winston.

Tomlinson, Carol Ann. 2014. *The Differentiated Classroom. Responding to the Needs of All Learners, 2nd Edition.* Reston, Virginia: Association for Supervision and Curriculum Development.

Van Tassel-Baska, Joyce. 2003. "Differentiating the Language Arts for High Ability Learners, K–8. ERIC Digest." Arlington, Virginia: ERIC Clearinghouse on Disabilities and Gifted Education.

Vygotsky, Lev Semenovich. 1978. "Interaction Between Learning and Development." *Mind in Society*, 79–91. Cambridge, Massachusetts: Harvard University Press.

Strategies for Using the Leveled Texts

Throughout this section are differentiation strategies that can be used with each leveled text to support reading comprehension for students in your classroom.

Below-Grade-Level Students

Peek-a-boo Picture Walk

As a prereading strategy, have students take a picture walk. Picture walks allow students to infer and make predictions about the text before viewing or reading the passage. This strategy allows below-grade-level students to activate prior knowledge before viewing or reading texts. Students should look at one picture at a time, covering the other three images. This technique allows students to focus on one image so they can pay close attention to details while examining each picture. During the picture walk, infuse as many text-specific words as possible into the classroom discussion. (A sample list can be found on page 134.) Additionally, use the sample questions below to focus the picture walk.

- What is happening in this picture?
- What do you think will happen next?
- What do you think this text is about?
- What other pictures might fit in this set?

Predict and Learn

In conjunction with the picture walk, students can write or sketch their predictions on the Predict and Learn chart below. This strategy requires below-grade-level students to actively analyze texts before viewing or reading them and provides a reference for classroom discussions afterwards.

What I predict	What I learned

Strategies for Using the Leveled Texts *(cont.)*

Below-Grade-Level Students *(cont.)*

Sequencing Graphic Organizer

The sequencing graphic organizer below can be used before, during, and/or after reading a text. Have students focus on what is happening at the beginning, middle, and end of a passage. This organizer can assist below-grade-level students in recalling the texts. Depending on students' abilities, entries can be sketched, labeled, and/or written.

Beginning

Middle

End

Oral Storytelling

As an alternative to completing the graphic organizer above, students can orally retell what they learned from a text. This is a great comprehension strategy for below-grade-level students because it allows them to engage with texts while building listening and speaking skills. Oral storytelling is a great way for teachers to informally assess students' understanding of texts. Students can be prompted with the following questions: What happened first? Then what happened?

133

Strategies for Using the Leveled Texts (cont.)

Below-Grade-Level Students (cont.)

Frontloading Word Bags

Frontloading, or pre-teaching, vocabulary is a powerful tool for this student population. This strategy allows students who are below grade level to access content within a text through discussions beforehand. This can be a useful tool for students who struggle with on-demand activities. Select words from the text and place them in a bag prior to reading or introducing the text to students. Label the front of the bag with the title of the passage. Students can then work in a group or with the teacher to pull words out and discuss them. All questions and discussions should be focused on vocabulary comprehension and synthesizing words as they pertain to the main idea of each text.

Text	Words, Themes, and Content
Animal Parents and Babies	penguin, egg, hen, chicks, animal, babies, father, mother, warms, shows, safe, protect
Shapes	wheel, circle, blocks, squares, roll, smoothly, stacked
Playing Sports	basketball, soccer, players, points, feet, field
Grandpa and Me	walk, read, park, bookstore, outside, favorite, interesting
Homes Around the World	apartment, yurt, home, apartment building, inside, family, entrance
Crafty Kids	picture frames, patterns, students, fundraise, attractive, buttons, purchase
Getting Ready for School	cereal, juice, bread, peanut butter, glass, eats, morning, dressed, breakfast, spreads, dishes
Our Favorite Sports	sports, graph, vote, show, popular, classroom, different, soccer, softball, kickball, data
Birthday Time!	friends, twins, birthday, party, together, invite, combine, total
Looking at Animals	python, snake, length, adult, stretching, bunching
Plenty of Plants!	plants, carrots, spinach, around, crunchy, leafy, healthy, tasty
The Seasons	spring, summer, autumn, winter, through, change, becomes
How Sound Moves	vibrate, sound waves, drummer, stick, quickly, travels
Light Makes a Rainbow	rain, light, bends, rainbow, through, causes
Tools	telescope, microscope, tool, space, clear
Be Fair!	fair, equal, treat, chances
Money	money, earn, pay, work, buy, bill, coin, job
Jobs Around Town	nurse, firefighters, doctors, types, care, help, safe
Getting Around School	school, map, key, places, show, symbol, landmarks, locate, find
Happy 4th of July, America!	July, celebrate, freedom, observed, independence, fourth, parades, holiday

Strategies for Using the Leveled Texts *(cont.)*

Below-Grade-Level Students *(cont.)*

Graphic Organizer to Find Similarities and Differences

Setting a purpose for reading content focuses the learner. One purpose for reading can be to identify similarities and differences. This skill must be directly taught, modeled, and applied. Use the texts in this book to further students' understanding and/or to allow them to demonstrate what they know about a topic. For example, students could compare and contrast the *Rules at Home* passage to the rules in their own homes. Discussion questions can be questions such as the following: How are the rules in your home like the ones in the text? How are they different? The chart below can be used to respond to these questions.

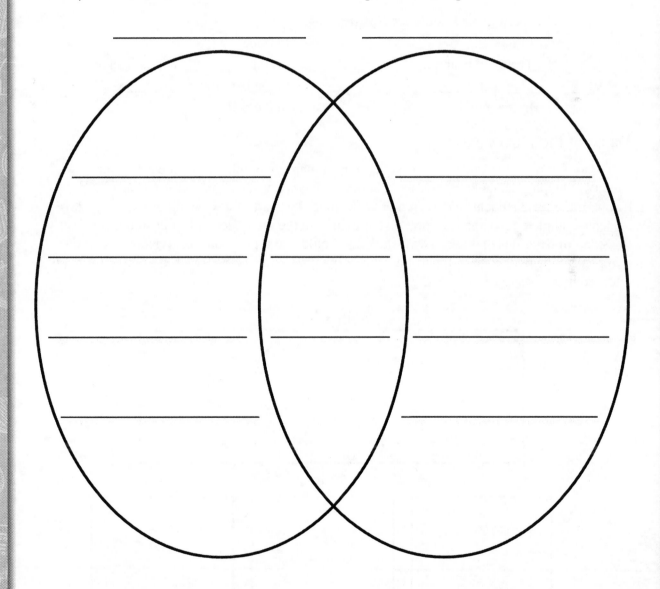

Strategies for Using the Leveled Texts *(cont.)*

Below-Grade-Level Students *(cont.)*

Sentence Frames

This is an underused technique that produces great results. Many below-grade-level students struggle with reading comprehension. They may need sentence frameworks to help them attack texts and gain confidence in discussing the material. Once students gain confidence and learn how to locate factual information, you phase out this technique.

There are two steps to successfully using this technique. First, use sentence prompts during discussions. Second, students use framed sentences when discussing and summarizing texts.

Examples of Sentence Frames

I think _____.   I notice _____.

The story is about _____.   I think _____ will happen next.

I learned _____.   In the beginning, _____.

In the middle, _____.   In the end, _____.

Mapping the Main Idea

For nonfiction texts, students can use main idea maps. Combining the ideas behind Creative Mapping (Naughton 1993) and Semantic Mapping (Pearson and Johnson 1978), below-grade-level students can sketch or write about texts after previewing or reading. Have students complete the largest section on the map with the main idea. Prompt students to use titles and illustrations to do so. Next, students should add representations (visual or written) to represent the details that support the main idea. This strategy can be used before, during, or after reading a passage.

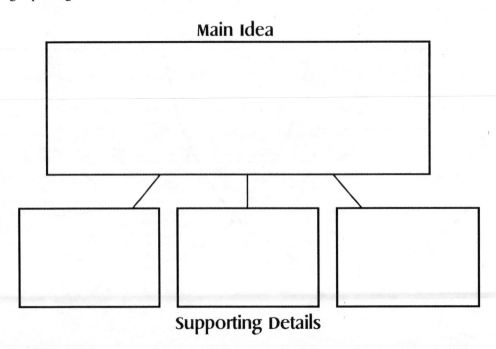

Main Idea

Supporting Details

Strategies for Using the Leveled Texts *(cont.)*

On-Grade-Level Students

Questioning

Questioning is a great way for students to check their reading comprehension. This strategy can be student or teacher driven. After reading each text, have students pull one of the words from a bag and use the word to pose a question about the text to a classmate. Here are sample questions for the texts in this book:

Who	takes care of animal babies?
What	patterns can you spot around us?
Where	do you live?
When	might you use a map?
Why	do we need tools?
How	can I earn and use money?

Question Bag

KWL

KWL charts empower students to take ownership of their learning. This strategy can be used as a pre- or post-reading tool for organizing what they've read or for further exploration for on-grade-level students. Guide students with the following questions:

What does scanning the text tell us?   What do you know about the topic?

What do you want to know about the topic?   What did you learn about the topic?

KWL Chart

What do I know? (K)	What do I want to learn? (W)	What did I learn? (L)

137

Strategies for Using the Leleled Texts *(cont.)*

Above-Grade-Level Students

Student-Directed Learning

Because they are academically advanced, above-grade-level students are often the leaders in primary classrooms. They are more self-sufficient learners, too. As a result, there are some student-directed strategies that teachers can employ successfully with these students. Remember to use the texts in this book as jump-starts so students will be interested in finding out more about the topics. Above-grade-level students may enjoy any of the following activities:

Reading and Writing Activities

- Write your own questions and exchange them with others.

- Craft your own story using the characters from the text.

- Read other texts about the topic to further expand your knowledge.

- Extend the plot of the story and write a new ending to the text.

- Research topics and write your own "All About" book.

Listening and Speaking Activities

- Read the text and teach the topic to another group of students.

- Interview a friend about the topic read.

Art Activities

- Draw and label a detailed diagram of what you learned.

- Make a hand puppet to act out and retell the story.

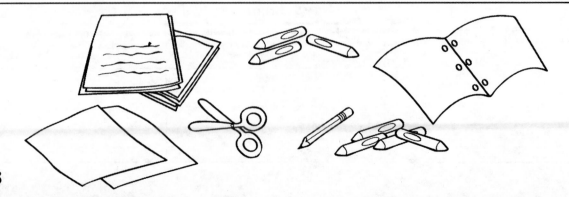

138

Strategies for Using the Leveled Texts *(cont.)*

Above-Grade-Level Students *(cont.)*

Open-Ended Questions and Activities

Teachers need to be aware of activities that provide a ceiling that is too low for above-grade-level students. When given activities like this, these students become disengaged. These students can do more, but how much more? Offering open-ended questions and activities will provide above-grade-level students with opportunities to perform at or above their ability levels. For example, ask students to analyze the content described in the texts, such as: "Explain several ways our lives are affected by the use of tools?" or "What is the best way to be fair when playing a game?" These questions require students to form opinions, think deeply about the issues, and form statements in their minds. To questions like this, there really is not one right answer.

The generic open-ended question stems listed here can be adapted to any topic. These question stems can be used to develop comprehension questions for the leveled texts in this book.

- In what ways did . . .
- How might you have done this differently . . .
- What if . . .
- What are some possible explanations for . . .
- How does this affect . . .
- Explain several reasons why . . .
- What problems does this create . . .

- Describe the ways . . .
- What is the best . . .
- What is the worst . . .
- What is the likelihood . . .
- Predict the outcome . . .
- Support your reason . . .
- Make a plan for . . .
- Propose a solution . . .

Strategies for Using the Leveled Texts *(cont.)*

Above-Grade-Level Students *(cont.)*

Extension Activities

Extension activities can be used with above-grade-level students to build independence. All of these suggested extension ideas are geared towards research, presentation, crafts, and writing to extend the texts through classwork or as home/school connection assignments. (Note: All the passages do not have extension activities.)

Text	Extension Activities
Animal Parents and Babies	Do you know of other animal parents that take care of their babies? Make a book explaining how these animals take care of their babies.
Shapes	What other shapes do you know? Make and label a poster to show five more shapes that you know.
Grandpa and Me	Interview one of your grandparents and present the information to your class.
Getting Ready for School	How do you get ready for school? Make a comic strip to show the steps you take.
Birthday Time!	Make a list of friends that you want to come to your next birthday party.
Looking at Animals	Research another animal using books in your class. Present the information to your class.
Plenty of Plants!	Treasure Hunt! Look in a newspapers or magazines. Find as many plant pictures you can find, then glue them to a poster board.
The Seasons	Which season do your classmates like best? Take a vote and make a graph to show the data.
Tools	What tools do you use in school? Make a list or draw a picture of all the tools you use to help you work at school.
Be Fair!	What are the rules in your house? Make a poster to show all of them.
Jobs Around Town	What job do you want when you grow up? Write about it, then make a picture to go with your writing.
Happy 4th of July, America	What holidays do you celebrate? Bring in artifacts from the holiday to show to your class.

Strategies for Using the Leveled Texts (cont.)

English Language Learners

Vocabulary Work

Building academic vocabulary is essential for English language learners. This strategy can be used before or after reading a text. Start your discussion for each text by asking students about each word that they will encounter in the text. Teachers can print the words and have a visual image of each word. Allowing English language leaners to encounter text prior to the on-demand activity will aid in fluency, build confidence, and allow students opportunities to process content and focus on comprehension rather than decoding while reading. A list of suggested vocabulary words from the texts in this book is included on page 134.

Picture Dictionary

As an extension to the vocabulary activity, students can make picture dictionaries. Illustrating text-specific words can help students make visual connections to words in the texts. As students are reading the texts, they can look at picture clues to assist with text meaning.

_____'s **Picture Dictionary**	_____	_____

Strategies for Using the Leveled Texts *(cont.)*

English Language Learners *(cont.)*

Practice Concepts and Language Objectives

English language learners need to practice what they learn through engaging activities. Some people retain knowledge better after applying what they learn to their own lives. This is definitely true for many English language learners. Students can apply content and language knowledge by creating projects, stories, skits, poems, or artifacts that show what they learned. Some activities should be geared to the right side of the brain, like those listed above. For students who are left-brain dominant, activities such as defining words and concepts, using graphic organizers, and explaining procedures should be developed.

Interview

Students may interview members of their families or neighbors to obtain information regarding a topic from the texts in this book. For example: What types of plants do you eat?

Home/School Connection

The home/school connection is an important component in the learning process for English language learners. Parents are students' first teachers, and they establish expectations for their children. These expectations help shape the behavior of their children. By asking parents to be active participants in the education of their children, students get double doses of support and encouragement. As a result, families become partners, and chances for success in your classroom increase. You can send home copies of the texts in this book for parents to read with their children. You can even send multiple levels to meet the needs of your second-language parents as well as your students. In this way, you are sharing what you are covering in class with your whole second-language community.

Strategies for Using the Leveled Texts *(cont.)*

English Language Learners *(cont.)*

Cause and Effect

This cause-and-effect graphic organizer will assist English language learners to "see" the relationships between causes and effects in the texts read. The texts and prompts below can be used to utilize this graphic organizer.

Text	Cause/Effect
Animal Parents and Babies	Animal parents take care of their babies . . .
Homes Around the World	If you move often . . .
Birthday Time!	Josh and Jen are having a birthday . . .
The Seasons	Spring is over . . .

Cause   **Effect**

Resources

Contents of Digital Resource CD

PDF Files

The full-color PDFs provided are each six pages long and contain all three levels of a reading passage. For example, *Animal Parents and Babies* PDF (pages 11–16) would be the *parentsbabies.pdf* file.

Text Files

The Microsoft Word® documents include the text for all three levels of each reading passage. For example, *Animal Parents and Babies* text (pages 11–16) would be the *parentsbabies.docx* file.

Text Title	Text File	PDF
Animal Parents and Babies	parentsbabies.docx	parentsbabies.pdf
Shapes	shapes.docx	shapes.pdf
Playing Sports	sports1.docx	sports1.pdf
Grandpa and Me	grandpa.docx	grandpa.pdf
Homes Around the World	homes.docx	homes.pdf
Crafty Kids	crafty.docx	crafty.pdf
Getting Ready for School	school.docx	school.pdf
Our Favorite Sports	sports2.docx	sports2.pdf
Birthday Time!	birthday.docx	birthday.pdf
Looking at Animals	animals.docx	animals.pdf
Plenty of Plants!	plants.docx	plants.pdf
The Seasons	seasons.docx	seasons.pdf
How Sound Moves	soundmoves.docx	soundmoves.pdf
Light Makes a Rainbow	rainbow.docx	rainbow.pdf
Tools	tools.docx	tools.pdf
Be Fair!	fair.docx	fair.pdf
Money	money.docx	money.pdf
Jobs Around Town	jobs.docx	jobs.pdf
Getting Around School	aroundschool.docx	aroundschool.pdf
Happy 4th of July, America!	4thofjuly.docx	4thofjuly.pdf

Word Documents of Texts

- Change leveling further for individual students.
- Separate text and images for students who need additional help decoding the text.
- Resize the text for visually impaired students.

Digital Resource CD

Full-Color PDFs of Texts

- Project texts for whole-class review.
- Post on your website and read texts online.
- Email texts to parents or students at home.